Rewards for hard work

This book belongs to

_____

Written by Stephen Barnett
Illustrated by Rosie Brooks

Contents

Rewards for hard work 3

Count to ten 17

New words 31

What did you learn? 32

About this book

Two stories which will motivate children to work hard and to control their anger are the highlight of this book. The simple style of story telling will surely catch the attention of the young readers and encourage them to read more and more.

Rewards for hard work

It was Saturday. My job for the weekend was to help my father in the garden. I was mowing the lawn. I wanted to complete the mowing quickly because there were many other interesting things that I wanted to do.

'Is it alright if I just mow the big middle part in the lawn,' I asked my father, 'and leave the edges for the next time?' My father thought for a while and came across to where I was standing.

'There is a saying, "if a job is worth doing, then it is worth doing well". This means that when you have a task, then you should do it to the very best of your ability. Then you will have pride in what you've done,' said father.

I could not understand what father said but I kept on mowing the lawn, though a little sadly.

After a little while, I began to see what my father had meant. The lawn looked lovely and tidy. Now I felt like doing some more work to make the garden look even better!

I started to pull out the weeds which grew around the flowers. I was so into my work that I didn't even notice the time!

My sister and my mother came to see what I was doing.
'I've never seen the lawn look so wonderful!' exclaimed my sister. 'You are doing a marvellous job. I didn't know that you could work so well!' said my mother. I was pleased and gave them a smile.

The woman who lived next door looked over the fence and saw what I was doing. 'That's a great job,' she said. 'When you've finished there, perhaps you'd like to come to my house and help me in my garden. I would be glad to pay you for your help.'

I continued through the afternoon, sweeping
paths, trimming hedges, making up compost
heaps.
My mother brought a glass of cold juice
for me. 'Here,' she said 'you should rest a bit
and drink this. You've done a wonderful job.'

12

I sat down for a moment and admired what I had done. I was satisfied with the result of my hard work as the garden looked clean and beautiful.

Later, when I had finished, my parents came to see the garden. It looked terrific and I was very proud. My mother looked around and said, 'I have never seen the garden look so beautiful! Thank you very much Paul, for making the extra effort and working so hard.'

A little later my father came. 'So, what do you think?'
'You were right,' I replied. 'It was lots of hard work but it was rewarding, and I liked doing it. And now I have the chance of doing it in return of money too!'

I learnt that day that hard work does have its rewards!

Count to ten

We were playing in the school playground after we had finished our lunch. We were playing a chasing game and so we were running across the school field. I was chasing Alan trying to tag him.

Suddenly a football zoomed across and
knocked onto Alan's back. 'Oof!' he called out.
He stopped and put his hand on his back. 'That
hurt!' he shouted, looking around to see where
the ball had come from.

'Sorry!' called out one of the boys as he approached to collect the ball. 'We were just having a kick-around. We didn't mean to hit you.'

'Well, you did hit me!' shouted Alan at the little
boy. Alan was angry. He ran forward to pick
up the ball before the other boy could get it.
'Please give him back the ball, Alan,' I said. 'It
was just an accident. And you're not so hurt!'

'No, I won't,' said Alan, and he kicked the ball right over the school fence onto the road! A car ran over the ball and squashed it flat. The ball was destroyed completely.

Just then, our teacher came to see what was happening. 'Why did you do that, Alan?' she asked. 'The ball hit me. It made me angry,' said Alan.
'I know that it gave you a surprise,' said the teacher, 'and it probably hurt for a moment. But it was an accident!'

'You lost your temper,' said the teacher, 'and now look what has happened. You have upset the other boys, the football game has come to a stop, and you have ruined someone's ball! All because you lost your temper!'

Alan was looking down at the ground and was quiet for a moment. Finally he looked up at the teacher. 'I'm sorry,' he said. 'Next time something like this happens, I will try to control my temper.'

Alan apologised to the small boy and said that he would get him another ball.

'That's better,' said our teacher. 'Now, I have an
idea for you. If you lose your temper another
time, can you count up to ten?'

Alan laughed, 'Of course I can! But what good would that do?'

'Well,' the teacher said, 'next time something like this happens and you feel yourself getting angry, slowly count to ten. You'll find that by the time you get to ten, your anger has disappeared!'

'Now when I am with Alan and something happens to annoy him, I see him stop and quietly count upto ten. And it works!'

New words

weekend
interesting
quickly
morning
edges
across
task
pride
ability
lawn
lovely
tidy
marvellous
wonderful
pleased
glad
fence
great
continued
compost
trimming
hedges
sweeping
admired
result

terrific
beautiful
proud
extra
rewarding
replied
rewards
chasing
tag
zoomed
knocked
hurt
approached
collect
forward
accident
moment
angry
temper
ruined
control
apologised
quietly

What did you learn?

Rewards for hard work
What was the boy's job for the weekend?
What did the mother bring to the boy for him to drink?
What is the boy's name?

Count to ten
What happened to the ball when Alan kicked it onto the road?
What colour is the teacher's hair?
What did the teacher tell Alan to do when he lost his temper?